DESPERATE PRAYER

Desperate Prayer

DESPERATE PRAYER

Jonathan Redden

Christian Year Publications

ISBN-13: 978 1 912522 50 7

Typeset by John Ritchie Ltd., Kilmarnock
Printed by Bell & Bain Ltd., Glasgow

ACKNOWLEDGEMENTS

I wish to thank all the Christian authors and preachers who have taught me. I am grateful to Alison Banks, Fraser Munro and Ritchie Christian Media for their kind help and patience. I thank God for Jane my wife who has helped me to understand more the practice of prayer.

Contents

Foreword

We all at times face 'desperate situations' in life, and at such times often resort to 'Desperate Prayers'. But does God hear those prayers? At such desperate times our faith in a sovereign and gracious God is so often challenged and we really wonder whether our Heavenly Father is really listening. The honest truth is that usually it is us who are not listening to God's answer. In the face of disappointment, tragedies, persistent problems, unexpected disaster or ill health, we so often cry out in desperation and expect or desire an instant answer from God, and when it does not come immediately, or the answer is not what we are looking for, our confidence and faith is so easily shattered. So what can we learn from God's Word about 'Desperate Prayer'?

Jonathan Redden has helpfully brought together a collection of wonderful examples from scripture of 'Desperate Prayers' and shows us what we can learn about a sovereign and gracious God in the way He responds to such 'Desperate Prayer'. This should not only give us a renewed confidence in our Heavenly Father, but also help us to understand that He is sovereign and does not always answer prayer in the way we would expect or wish for. It is all too easy to rejoice when God answers our 'Desperate Prayers with a 'Yes', but can we still trust Him when the answer is 'No'? Whatever God's answer, we need to be reminded that God is good at all times, even when the answer is not what we are looking for. We need to remember our Lord's 'Desperate Prayer' in the garden of Gethsemane, where He prayed *"Father, if it is Your will, take this cup away from Me; nevertheless not My will, but Yours, be done."* (Luke 22.42). Where would we be today, if our Lord had not drunk that bitter cup to the very end?

'Desperate Prayers' are intensely personal, and God's response is also intensely personal. Prayer is a two-way process between our Lord and us, and the examples in this helpful little book can both challenge us and encourage us in our prayer life to trust in a sovereign, gracious and omnipotent God. Nonetheless, 'Desperate Prayer' is never easy! We so often find ourselves in impossible situations with no obvious way forward. At such times we can learn from King Jehoshaphat when he was facing the vast armies of the Moabites and Ammonites (2 Chronicles 20.12) and he could cry out that 'Desperate Prayer' –*"For we have no power against this great multitude that is coming against us; nor do we know what to do, but our eyes are upon You.".* God answered that prayer in a remarkable way, and so when we face desperate situations, let us also resort to 'Desperate Prayer', knowing and trusting that our sovereign and gracious Lord will not only hear our prayers, but will answer them in a way that will be to our ultimate blessing and His glory. At such times let us also echo another 'Desperate Prayer' – *"Lord, I believe; help my unbelief"* (Mark 9.24).

W. E. G. Thomas MS FRCS
Former President of The Gideons International
Former Consultant Surgeon and Vice President of the Royal
College of Surgeons

Preface

The Lord is good,
A stronghold in the day of trouble;
And He knows those who trust in Him.
Nahum 1:7

There are many books on prayer. Authors write prayers for numerous occasions. They advise on how we approach prayer, and what prayers are valid. They recommend a helpful frame of mind, the type of place, and what posture we should adopt, when and for how long we should pray. They instruct us in the content of our prayers. Yet even with all this helpful work, we have to admit that prayer is a difficult discipline for many of us. We often relegate it to times when we do not have anything specific to do. Some have even given up on prayer.

After seeing Jesus in the practice of prayer, His disciples noticed that something very wonderful was going on. Jesus seemed to be at ease with prayer and had a natural relationship with His Father. It is not surprising that they asked Him, "Lord, teach us to pray" (Luke 11:1).

At church services and prayer meetings, some seem to be clear and fluent, and others seem to be stuttering and nervous. In spite of all the books and examples, it is clear that few of us are at ease with prayer. When we read prayers, they sometimes become routine and we go through the motions. At other times, our minds wander and fail to keep on the subject of our prayer and God Himself seems to be remote.

Few of us feel ourselves to be experts in the many categories of prayer, but every one of us is an expert in desperate prayer. They are uttered at any time and in all places. They occur when the situation is acute, deteriorating and there appears to be an inevitable poor outcome. Even those who profess no particular religion will say, "God, help me!"

We have all been in these circumstances and afterwards, we have forgotten that we prayed or have failed to realise how God answered it.

My interest in desperate prayer began when I uttered the most desperate prayer of my life.

Up to that time, many regarded my life as being successful. As a surgeon, nearly every day was an intellectual and technical challenge with successes and occasional disappointments.

Not long after my late wife, Ros, had developed cancer, I contracted a rare autoimmune disease called granulomatosis with polyangitis. Like her, my treatment consisted of chemotherapy using anti cancer type medication.

I felt ill and able to do little for week after week and month after month.

Eventually I blurted out some prayers, one of which went like this:

"Lord, I know You love me and I love You. Either, take me to be with You or make me better, but I cannot serve You like this!"

It appeared that I wanted death more than that state of ill-health.

Two weeks later, I started to feel better. I was then able to nurse my wife during her last few months, which was very special for both of us. She died full of faith.

During the following eleven years, I have remarried, attended Bible College, played golf, walked the dog, been involved in Christian work and go on holidays. I am still learning how to pray.

I would venture to say that God loves to hear our desperate prayers. One of the reasons is that it is the time when we are real and there is no pretence.

In the Bible, great women and men of God have uttered desperate prayers. They were faced with tough decisions just as we are. Like us, their prayers were answered in varying ways. The answers to those prayers were not always immediate. Sometimes, it was yes, sometimes wait, and at other times the answer was no. Frequently, the answer was unexpected.

This short volume contains some of those prayers. I have included the ones I have found the most thought-provoking. I have included those prayers that are on the whole short. Since many preachers and writers have commented on the Psalms, I have not included them in this series. The Psalms are full of desperate prayers which deserve a fuller separate treatment.

The following sections can be read individually or in clusters. They are for private or group study. Far from descending into gloom, I pray that those who read them will be encouraged in every aspect of their lives.

Finally, it has to be remembered that, with notable exceptions, desperate prayer is often selfish. Following these prayers, many Biblical characters turned from being self-centred to being God-centred.

God is Just

*And Cain said to the Lord, "My punishment is greater than
I can bear! Surely You have driven me out this day from the
face of the ground; I shall be hidden from Your face; I shall be a
fugitive and a vagabond on the earth, and it will happen that
anyone who finds me will kill me."*
Genesis 4:13

For the first entry, it has to be admitted that this quote
can hardly be regarded as a prayer. It is not uttered from
an attitude of faith but of faithless complaint. It shows how
that from the beginning of our race, there is a complete
example of unbelief and rebellion.

Cain had been perfunctory with his worship of God. He
was flooded with jealousy and envy of his brother Abel.
He murdered his brother and this was followed by a lie
and a total lack of remorse.

And then, when deserving of severe punishment, he
complained that his sentence was too hard!

His attitude is echoed by many atheist critics.

They spend their lives ignoring God's ways. They claim
that because we are here by accident and blind chance,

there is no such thing as right and wrong and yet they howl with moral indignation at what they perceive to be God's judgments.

The lack of logic is amazing.

They rightly criticize the failings and sins of Christians and Christian institutions yet at the same time appear to discount the atrocities of atheist-inspired regimes from those of Stalin, Mao Zedong, Enver Hoxha to Pol Pot .

God's punishment of Cain was remarkably gracious. It gave him an opportunity to repent, but there was no indication that he ever did.

There is a reminder for us in the prayer Jesus taught us:

And forgive us our debts,
As we forgive our debtors.
And do not lead us into temptation,
But deliver us from the evil one.
(Matthew 6:12-13)

The Christian life begins and continues with repentance.

Prayer

Father, help me to realize when I do wrong. I will never make excuses, but ask for Your forgiveness. Thank You that You are just, loving and forgiving.

God Knows All About Me

Then she called the name of the Lord who spoke to her, You-Are-the-God-Who-Sees; for she said, "Have I also here seen Him who sees me?"
Genesis 16:13

Everything went wrong with Hagar's relationship with Sarai her mistress. God promised Abram that his wife would bear a son and that he would be a father of many nations. As time went by and nothing was happening, Sarai thought that her maid-servant Hagar would be a good surrogate.

That was the first of a series of mistakes. The second mistake was Abram's agreement. He should have realised that he needed to be patient and wait for the fulfilment of God's plan. He should have anticipated that the proposed arrangement would lead to rivalry and jealousy. The third mistake was Hagar's change of attitude when, on conceiving, she began to despise Sarai. The fourth mistake was Sarai's harsh treatment of Hagar leading to Hagar's flight into a precarious world.

When at the end of her tether, Hagar sat by a spring and wept. At this point she experienced a visitation by the

Angel of the Lord. This would be an appearance of the pre-incarnate Christ.

Following the promise of the Angel of the Lord concerning her son, she had a realization of God's wonderful grace. She felt a profound sense of God's awareness and overriding care when she called out her prayer of distress. She realised in a beautiful phrase that God is the one who sees everything and everyone including her.

When we have made misjudged and thoughtless choices and everything starts to go wrong, it is then we need to know that God knows and God cares. It may not be clear at the time, but when the way appears to become worse and hazardous, God will see us through now and for eternity. Hagar returned to her mistress. Her situation was not solved and she was evicted again, and yet God's hand was on her life. When we go from one disaster to another, it may not be obvious at the time, but God remains as "The God who sees".

The Bible is full of stories of how God deals faithfully with people who undergo repeated calamity and yet emerge chastened and even better than before.

> *O Lord, You have searched me and known me.*
> *You know my sitting down and my rising up;*
> *You understand my thought afar off.*
> *You comprehend my path and my lying down,*
> *And are acquainted with all my ways.*
> *For there is not a word on my tongue,*
> *But behold, O Lord, You know it altogether.*
> (Psalm 139:1-4)

Prayer

You see me, Lord. You know everything about me. Help me to realize that I cannot deceive You but instead rejoice in Your guidance.

Can We Bargain with God?

Then Jacob made a vow, saying, "If God will be with me, and
keep me in this way that I am going, and give me bread to eat
and clothing to put on, so that I come back to my father's house
in peace, then the Lord shall be my God. And this stone which I
have set as a pillar shall be God's house, and of all that You give
me I will surely give a tenth to You."
Genesis 28:20-22

Jacob fled from Canaan because he had tricked his elder brother Esau out of his birthright. Jacob was unpromising material as a patriarch for the people of God, and an unlikely source of God's blessing. He was selfish, a trickster and schemer. To use a modern example, "You would not want to buy a second-hand car from this man."

And yet God used him, and as his life continued through all its trials, God shaped him, albeit slowly, into the man he needed to be.

This desperate prayer was a beginning. It followed his vision of a ladder extending from earth to heaven. It demonstrates a type of prayer that we often utter at the dawn of our Christian journey. It is a conditional prayer. "If You do this and make my life successful, then I will trust in You." Alternatively, "If I come out of this mess, then I will believe in You!"

Some people use God as a lucky charm to manage life's problems and then fall away when tough things happen.

Jacob's promise had a positive aspect when he promised to give a tenth of all that he owned to God. He had started on a road that in the end made Jacob realize that God is Lord of everything and owns everything.

God is the one we should serve whatever the outcome. He is God and it should be our joy to realize that we should stop bargaining and trust Him. Ultimately, no matter the trial and suffering, He will save us and do and be the best for us, and His people.

Centuries later when the great, cruel Babylonian threat hung over Judah, the prophet Habakkuk realized what unconditional faith and trust really meant.

> *Though the fig tree may not blossom,*
> *Nor fruit be on the vines;*
> *Though the labour of the olive may fail,*
> *And the fields yield no food;*
> *Though the flock may be cut off from the fold,*
> *And there be no herd in the stalls —*
> *Yet I will rejoice in the Lord,*
> *I will joy in the God of my salvation.*
> *The Lord God is my strength;*
> *He will make my feet like deer's feet,*
> *And He will make me walk on my high hills.*
> (Habakkuk 3:17-19)

Prayer

Thank You that You can welcome people like Jacob. May we grow in our understanding and commitment.

The Changed Man

I will not let You go unless You bless me!
Genesis 32:26

Years previously, Jacob had tricked his elder brother out of his birthright and now was about to meet him. Esau had four hundred men with him and could easily have destroyed Jacob and his family. That night, having sent the family, servants, flocks and cattle over the river in groups to give an impression of power, he wrestled with a Man all night. There is a deeper sense here that Jacob was wrestling with God, for the Man was the Angel of the Lord. This was Christ Himself.

At the end of it Jacob uttered the above despairing prayer. When we pray, God always answers our prayer. It may not be immediate. It may not be what we want or expect. We may not even see benefit or purpose, but answer it He does.

God answered the prayer by giving Jacob a new name, Israel. Jacob means "trickster", whereas Israel means, "one who struggles with God".

His descendants, as a nation, were God's chosen people but so often struggled with God and their destiny.

God also answered the prayer in softening Esau's heart which led to a cordial and even affectionate meeting.

However, as part of that night's struggle, Jacob/Israel had been bruised in his hip joint and limped for the rest of his life. He never forgot this encounter. Jacob became a repentant man who began to see that he had to put God first in his life, rather than try to manipulate God into making life easy and a success on his own terms.

Sometimes God allows us to suffer in order to show that He can trust us for bigger things. The Christian who has suffered is often more in a position to help others in their difficulties. The Christian who has suffered fractures sympathizes in a real way with those suffering physical trauma. The Christian who has undergone chemotherapy understands those who are presented with a diagnosis of life-threatening cancer.

God sometimes allows Christians to experience hard lessons, but in the end these tough lessons lead to blessing.

Furthermore, we may, like Jacob, have to learn God's ways the hard way. Paul knew all about that when he wrote his letter to a wayward church:

Do not be deceived, God is not mocked; for whatever a man sows, that he will also reap. For he who sows to his flesh will of the flesh reap corruption, but he who sows to the Spirit will of the Spirit reap everlasting life. And let us not grow weary while doing good, for in due season we shall reap if we do not lose heart. (Galatians 6: 7-9)

Prayer

Father, may we always realize that Your love is with us all the time and that we can trust You in every part of our lives.

Please Send Someone Else!

*But he said, "O my Lord, please send by the hand of whomever
else You may send."*
Exodus 4:13

This utterance is the equivalent of saying, "Please send
someone else." It comes at the end of a dialogue between
God and Moses. Moses, from infancy, had spent forty years
in the court of Pharaoh and then forty years in obscurity.
At that time, he was probably the most highly-educated
man in the world. He then received his vocation to lead
God's people out of slavery in Egypt.

Moses' first excuse was that they might not believe
him. The second was that he did not consider himself to
be eloquent. Finally, in spite of all his natural gifts and
anointing, he asked God to send someone else.

God's call is difficult to define, but faithful Christians
always are given a task to do. It may come through
circumstance, or a unique spiritual experience, or by clear
inner conviction.

There are clear examples in the Bible and subsequent
Christian history of reluctant servants. God is frequently
patient and gives us a further chance to say, "Yes", and take

up His call. However, if we continue to say, "No", then He will move on to another who will take on His cause. Later in the Bible we read of King Saul who fell away, and was replaced by David who was described as a man after God's own heart.

Moses was given Aaron as a mouthpiece and assistant in his leadership. In a way this was helpful but in other ways, Aaron was a disappointment.

There are many half-hearted Christians, who live out their lives in a one dimensional, dry, ineffective way because they said, "No!", to God. The usual cause of saying "No!" is somewhat like that of Moses. They are fearful and just want to go with the flow. We are advised to lead our lives in accordance with the natural and spiritual gifts that God has given us, no more, no less. We should neither exaggerate our abilities, nor should we minimize them The Apostle Paul summed up the situation perfectly:

For I say, through the grace given to me, to everyone who is among you, not to think of himself more highly than he ought to think, but to think soberly, as God has dealt to each one a measure of faith. For as we have many members in one body, but all the members do not have the same function, so we, being many, are one body in Christ, and individually members of one another. Having then gifts differing according to the grace that is given to us, let us use them: if prophecy, let us prophesy in proportion to our faith; or ministry, let us use it in our ministering; he who teaches, in teaching; he who exhorts, in exhortation; he who gives, with liberality; he who leads, with diligence; he who shows mercy, with cheerfulness. (Romans 12:3-8)

Prayer

We are all good at giving excuses for failing to serve You. Help us to say, "Yes!", when we know that You are leading us in a certain direction and not think that someone else will do.

The God of Forgiveness

Then Moses returned to the Lord and said, "Oh, these people have committed a great sin, and have made for themselves a god of gold! Yet now, if You will forgive their sin—but if not, I pray, blot me out of Your book which You have written."
Exodus 32:31-32

Israel, led by Moses, had escaped from Egypt across the Red Sea with accompanying signs and wonders from God.

They then began their journey and wanderings through the desert wilderness.

Moses had been some time away on Mount Sinai preparing the law and "ten commandments". On his return Moses was greeted with sounds of revelry and the idolatrous worship of a golden calf.

Moses was angry and fell before God in desperate, heart-rending prayer. He established right at the beginning that Israel had committed a great sin. Then comes an astonishing request that God would forgive their sin and if necessary kill him as a punishment.

I do not know anyone who has prayed that they

are prepared to die on account of another's fault. Paul expressed a similar sentiment in his epistle to the Romans:

I tell the truth in Christ, I am not lying, my conscience also bearing me witness in the Holy Spirit, that I have great sorrow and continual grief in my heart For I could wish that I myself were accursed from Christ for my brethren, my countrymen according to the flesh. (Romans 9:1-3)

Paul was grieving over the fact that the Jews in the main had rejected Jesus and he was even prepared to lose his own salvation if it meant that they would turn to their Messiah in faith.

The ultimate sacrifice was that of Jesus who suffered punishment, shame and death on a cross on behalf of the sins of His own people and sufficient for the whole world.

Suffering, death and punishment for sin are difficult issues for modern Western liberal humanity to face, let alone on behalf of others!

Yet Moses, Paul and Jesus describe the dreadfulness of sin. Christ, in particular, demonstrated His love in securing a remedy.

Philip Bliss made the point poignantly in his hymn:

Bearing shame and scoffing rude,
in my place condemned He stood,
sealed my pardon with His blood:
Hallelujah, what a Saviour!

Moses' prayer is not necessarily one to be copied but it speaks profoundly to every generation of believers.

Prayer

Dear God, many do not believe in You, help us to be for others what You want us to be. If necessary, help us to suffer for others.

The God of Glory

And he said, "Please, show me Your glory."
Exodus 33:18

This cry of the heart was spoken after successive crises during Israel's wandering in the Sinai wilderness. Moses had faced rebellion following the golden calf incident. This had resulted in the forceful restoration of order associated with thousands of deaths. Israel was a rebellious nation and yet God continued His forgiveness and guidance. In his prayer struggle with God, Moses sought reassurance.

There may have been a sense of insecurity which led to the entreaty, "Show me Your glory."

That world was filled with a panoply of gods which attracted so many people with their gold and false glitter. Moses and only a few faithful companions had remained faithful to the one true transcendent creator God. He needed a big dose of encouragement.

God answered his prayer by passing over Moses who had withdrawn to a cleft in the rock. Moses was only given a back view so to speak, but this was sufficient. A full view would have been utterly overwhelming and more than any could survive.

The New Testament fulfilled Moses' request when Jesus was transfigured on the mount. (Luke 9: 28-36)

Paul also referred to the glory which each Christian is able to witness through the agency of the Holy Spirit:

Nevertheless when one turns to the Lord, the veil is taken away. Now the Lord is the Spirit; and where the Spirit of the Lord is, there is liberty. But we all, with unveiled face, beholding as in a mirror the glory of the Lord, are being transformed into the same image from glory to glory, just as by the Spirit of the Lord. (2 Corinthians 3:16-18)

The Christian is often in need of reassurance, particularly after a life crisis. So often in such circumstances, nothing good or helpful happens and we are tempted to seek worldly solace in drink, drugs or some other pleasure. At this point, God allows us to pray, "Show me something of Your Glory. Help me know that You are real." Often, as in Moses' case, He answers in unexpected ways, but usually it is through an increased understanding and relationship with Jesus Himself.

As Paul indicates above, in the ancient world, mirrors were generally unclear or tarnished. At present our grasp and vision of God lacks full clarity, no matter what our spiritual state happens to be. One day, our understanding will be complete when we see Him face to face. (1 Corinthians 13:12, 1 John 3:2) What a glory! What a promise!

Prayer

Thank You, Father, that we see representations of Your glory in creation, in the Bible and most wonderfully in our Lord Jesus Christ.

Complaints Against God

Moses heard the people weeping throughout their families, all at the entrances of their tents. Then the Lord became very angry, and Moses was displeased. So Moses said to the Lord, "Why have you treated your servant so badly? Why have I not found favor in your sight, that you lay the burden of all this people on me? Did I conceive all this people? Did I give birth to them, that you should say to me, 'Carry them in your bosom, as a nurse carries a sucking child, to the land that you promised on oath to their ancestors'? Where am I to get meat to give to all this people? For they come weeping to me and say, 'Give us meat to eat!' I am not able to carry all this people alone, for they are too heavy for me. If this is the way you are going to treat me, put me to death at once—if I have found favor in your sight—and do not let me see my misery."
Numbers 11:10-15

The burden of leadership that had fallen on Moses had led to a descent into depression. Those who are given the mantle of leadership and responsibility often expect to be different from their predecessors and that their plans will bring about success. Rarely is this the case. The challenges facing all leaders including Christian leaders may be associated with crisis and self-doubt. It is easy to descend into blame and resentment, the feeling that others had failed, and let you down.

History has judged Moses to be one of the world's greatest leaders whose contribution is still felt to this day, and yet sometimes he wished that he was dead. To be fair, Moses did not seek command, but he did pin the blame on God for choosing Israel and appointing him to lead them to the Promised Land. It is easy to blame God for the dilemmas that are man-made.

Israel complained that the manna provided by God was not enough, even though it had been daily sustenance for the whole population. The troublemakers complained that they would have preferred slavery in Egypt. They wanted meat and other tasty morsels.

God's answer to this crisis prayer was wonderful in its patience and practicality. God did not upbraid Moses for his complaint against Him. He suggested that all the elders of Israel should be involved in a shared governance. The devolution of authority was timely and appropriate for the situation. However, the new leaders were to be given a portion of God's Spirit just as Moses had been given. As in churches today, it was important that they should all be united in their present and future plans.

The judgment that fell on Israel, associated with a glut of birds that had descended from the sky, is demonstrative of our need to be thankful for the sufficient resources that God supplies.

God gave manna in the wilderness. Jesus used this

history when He said that the Israelites ate manna and later died. The bread that Jesus offers is for eternal life:

I am the bread of life. Your fathers ate the manna in the wilderness, and are dead. This is the bread which comes down from heaven, that one may eat of it and not die. I am the living bread which came down from heaven. If anyone eats of this bread, he will live forever. (John 6:48-51)

Christians can become restless about the wonderful gift of Himself that Jesus is to us. They become obsessed with extras and add-ons. Just as manna was sufficient for the Israelites, so Christ and Him alone is more than sufficient for the Christian.

Prayer

Dear God, may I never grumble about You. May I find Jesus all sufficient. Thank You for supplying our daily needs.

Disaster Prevented

Then Joshua tore his clothes, and fell to the earth on his face
before the ark of the Lord until evening, he and the elders of
Israel; and they put dust on their heads. And Joshua said, "Alas,
Lord God, why have You brought this people over the Jordan at
all — to deliver us into the hand of the Amorites, to destroy us?
Oh, that we had been content, and dwelt on the other side of the
Jordan! O Lord, what shall I say when Israel turns its back before
its enemies? For the Canaanites and all the inhabitants of the
land will hear it, and surround us, and cut off our name from the
earth. Then what will You do for Your great name?"
Joshua 7:6-9

Following Israel's passage over Jordan, they defeated and destroyed Jericho. The next battle at Ai was marred by a serious setback. The reason for this originated with the sin of Achan. (Ch. 7:1)

Joshua was distraught. The initial success was now put in doubt and the whole campaign was facing military disaster. As usual in human affairs, God, in some way, was blamed for their predicament. (v.7)

In spite of this failure, the Elders kept a measure of faith in God, and remained loyal to Joshua.

After the prayer, God commanded Joshua to stand up and then deal with the sin that had affected the army. It was the problem of looting. This has been present throughout military history and here had changed victory into defeat.

Few of us are caught up in military calamities but we all have to face personal disasters.

They may be failure of exams, and unfulfilled expectations. It could be bereavement, loss of a job or divorce. There may be fault on our part, there may be no fault.

In the utterance of desperate prayer we usually ask God to intervene in some way and fix it. On this occasion as so often, the initiative was with the believer. Joshua was told to, "Stand up!" and deal with the sin that was affecting the whole of Israel.

When faced with life's problems, instead of heaping blame on others we have to ask ourselves, "What can I do?" Others may indeed be responsible but it is in accepting change in my actions, or my habits that help alter circumstances and attitudes. It may mean changing certain parts of our lifestyle, avoiding seemingly harmless pastimes, choosing a different group of friends.

None of these choices are easy but, as in Joshua's case, doing nothing is not an option.

There was once a young Christian who just managed to get to university. However, during this progress he always failed something in any series of exams. This usually caused some stress and uncertainty. So the young man prayed and vowed to God that he would not play cricket or do course study on a Sunday. After that, he never failed an exam.

Now this may seem to be appropriate for him alone but he felt that God honoured that discipline. It also meant that other things fitted into a structured programme.

Hard spiritual decisions bring their rewards. As we will see later, sometimes the way is painful, and the outcomes are not necessarily those that we prefer.

Prayer

Father, I pray that I will never criticize Your just and gentle rule. Help me to realize the things that I can do to remedy dangerous circumstances and the ability to carry them out.

The Danger of Idolatry

And the children of Israel cried out to the Lord, saying, "We
have sinned against You, because we have both forsaken our
God and served the Baals!"
Judges 10:10

This confession is the third collective acknowledgement
of sin recorded in the Bible. After the occupation of the
Promised Land, Israel practised a fantasy of idolatry that
was repeatedly warned against prior to their entry. Not
only have I sinned, but, "We have sinned."

Baal worship involved veneration of the sun god and
the god of storms. They were fertility gods and were
associated with crop production. The worship was allied
with idolatry, sensuality, temple prostitution and even
adult and child sacrifice.

Before the exile into Babylon, both Israel and Judah
repeatedly fell into this appalling idolatry, reaching its
heights during the reigns of Ahab and Jezebel.

The consequences of this led to family breakdown and
defeat by neighbouring enemies and, above all, God's
utter detestation. The Apostle Paul tells us that all idolatry
is ultimately devil worship. (1 Corinthians 10:20)

Humans are very good at manufacturing idols. Anything in the human heart that is in a place above God is an idol. Today, many people say they have no religion, or describe themselves as "Nones". However, they may have statues of Buddha or a Hindu deity in their homes. Garden centres sell these sculptures, and these sculptures are often found in prominent places. Although people say they are there as a decoration, they are an indication of a deep spiritual malaise or misunderstanding.

People make idols of their desires, pastimes, prestige, money and power. We all easily drift into the wrong priorities. Is it little wonder that our Lord Jesus taught us to say?

> *And do not lead us into temptation,*
> *But deliver us from the evil one.*
> (Matthew 6:13)

The Israelites were instructed to get rid of their foreign gods. They did that and were given forgiveness, victory and increased security. However, as we continue to read Israel's history, we soon discover that the reforms were not totally complete and, for the most part, were just short-lived.

On a personal note, years ago, we received an ornament which looked like a small Buddha. It was put on the kitchen mantelpiece with a number of other decorative and useful items. Not long after, we opened the kitchen door and found that it was the only ornament to have smashed to the floor. We realized that our house, God's house, was not to be shared with other gods. Instead of being disappointed, we were thankful.

Let's get rid of dubious ornaments, pictures and habits that take away God's first place in our lives. God has given us many things to enjoy. It is our perspective that can go wrong.

Prayer

In forsaking You, the Israelites went after other gods. Give your people the desire and Your power to put You first in their lives.

A Prayer for a Child

*And she was in bitterness of soul, and prayed to the Lord
and wept in anguish. Then she made a vow and said, "O
Lord of hosts, if You will indeed look on the affliction of
Your maidservant and remember me, and not forget Your
maidservant, but will give Your maidservant a male child, then
I will give him to the Lord all the days of his life, and no razor
shall come upon his head."*
1 Samuel 1:10-11

Hannah was a wife in a bigamous relationship. Her husband's other wife had children but Hannah was infertile. Although there were men of God in the Old Testament who were polygamous, these family structures were not part of God's original design for marriage. These arrangements were usually accompanied by poor and sadly, disastrous outcomes.

Infertility is a worldwide problem affecting 10-15% of couples and is frequently combined with anguish, anxiety, depressions, marital disharmony and feelings of worthlessness. Hannah's problem was made worse by the chiding of Peninnah, her rival.

Rather than descend into a downhill spiral, she sought

God in her distress. She made a covenant with God and asked for a male child. This was followed by unuttered prayer which Eli the priest thought was indicative of drunkenness!

Hannah rightly, as a strong woman, protested her innocence, and Eli finally urged her to go in peace, hoping that God would grant her desire.

The Bible then makes an interesting comment. Hannah returned home no longer downcast. She had come to terms with her situation and trusted God for the future.

In a short time she conceived and gave birth to Samuel, one of the great prophets of the Old Testament.

Our circumstances may cause deep anxiety which is reflected in our facial appearance. In the case of infertility there are many modern treatments. Nevertheless, the problem is not always solvable.

Whatever our problem, we should seek God in achieving a practical solution. In every case we can bring our trials before God. We can trust Him and take courage, that whatever the consequences, we have the knowledge and confidence that He is in ultimate control.

The result may not be what we expect. In Luke's Gospel there is a short piece about an old lady named Anna. Decades previously she had been married for seven years before her husband died. We are not told she had children and it is likely that they were an infertile couple. She did not fall into misery and self pity, she served God in the Temple and was a lovely lady of prayer. Ultimately, she was rewarded by seeing the infant Jesus. Whatever happens to us, and whatever anguish we have to face, those who trust Him will one day see Jesus face to face.

For now we see in a mirror, dimly, but then face to face. Now I know in part, but then I shall know just as I also am known. (1 Corinthians 13: 12)

Prayer

As Hannah wept for a child she later committed to You, we pray that our children will not dishonour You in the way Eli's did but seek to follow You in the way of Samuel.

Who is King of Your Life?

*Then all the elders of Israel gathered together and came to
Samuel at Ramah, and said to him, "Look, you are old, and
your sons do not walk in your ways. Now make us a king to
judge us like all the nations." But the thing displeased Samuel
when they said, "Give us a king to judge us." So Samuel prayed
to the Lord.*
1 Samuel 8:4-6

We are not told the contents of Samuel's prayer but we
can imagine the dire emergency situation that he faced
when the elders made their request with all its explicit and
implied criticism.

Samuel had judged Israel for years. He travelled on a
circuit and held court in the various towns. He administered
justice impartially and without favour. At this point, we
need to understand that it is Judeo Christianity that has
given the world an enormous gift. That is, the idea of
equality under the law. Sadly, Samuel's sons did not follow
their father's example and descended into corruption.

Not only was Samuel a judge, and a prophet, he was also
a political leader, making decisions for the nation. Although
a leader, he shunned the title and trappings of kingship.

He emphasized that as far as Israel was concerned, God was their king.

And yet, Israel wanted to copy other nations and appoint a king. This meant that Samuel would have to hand over the reins of administration to another who would exercise power in a very different way.

Although we are not told Samuel's words of prayer, we are told God's response. Here we see Samuel's intimate relationship with God and that prayer is a two-way process. We may not hear God speaking directly but during prayer we can often sense God's response. That is why it is wise to pray in a quiet place and accompany prayer with the reading of Scripture, even and particularly in an emergency situation. Many Christians can testify of how when feeling trapped in urgent circumstances, they have prayed, and then risen up from prayer with the knowledge of what should be done next.

Often we feel that in our lives and witness, people have disliked us and shunned us for one reason or another. Whilst we may well have made mistakes, in verse 7 we are reminded that it is not necessarily we that are being rejected, but it is because they know we are Christians, and it is that which people may reject. In fact, it is God who is being rejected. (v.7) Jesus said:

"If the world hates you, you know that it hated Me before it hated you. If you were of the world, the world would love its own. Yet because you are not of the world, but I chose you out of the world, therefore the world hates you. (John 15:18-19)

Samuel's address to Israel should be more widely understood and noted by all including those who exercise power. (vvs. 10-18)

In the end, Israel was given a king. Initially, this was a success but on continued reading we see a gradual fall towards disaster. This was only remedied by King Saul's replacement, David, whose reign brought in a golden age.

Prayer

Guide us we pray to respect whoever has authority over us in the secular world. Give us the grace and wisdom to understand the primacy of Your authority.

A Grievous Regret

Now the word of the Lord came to Samuel, saying, "I greatly regret that I have set up Saul as king, for he has turned back from following Me, and has not performed My commandments." And it grieved Samuel, and he cried out to the Lord all night.
1 Samuel 15:10-11

Saul's reign began with promise. He was from a humble background and was intelligent, tall and good-looking. He seemed to be just the man for the job. However, as time went by, inherent character flaws came to the front and led to his downfall. One of his problems was that his desire for worldly success and celebration took over from obedience to God. I have noticed a number of people who have put their career before anything else including their Christian development and relationship with God. The results have been a spiritually stunted and sometimes embittered middle and old age. Jesus said:

For what will it profit a man if he gains the whole world, and loses his own soul? Or what will a man give in exchange for his soul? (Mark 8:36-37)

In the end, Saul lost his soul. This loss was accompanied

by episodes of severe depression and fits of rage. Ultimately, he consulted a medium and committed suicide in battle by falling on his sword.

Samuel was only too well aware of Saul's weakness, and he cried to God all night. Parents and friends have seen deterioration of their nearest and dearest. Many nights have been spent in prayer and weeping before God. And yet for all that sorrow and grieving, we have to arrive at a state of acceptance. A severe warning to that much-loved close friend may be necessary. These events are as hard to bear as they are puzzling. After all that work, concern and prayer, "Why does God allow this?"

Samuel had to accept that God had finally rejected Saul. He had to come to terms with the fact that Saul wanted to suit himself rather than be obedient to God, and as a consequence, Saul was responsible for his own downfall.

The answer to the question, "Why?" is difficult to know, but ultimately God is in control and He has the last word.

And I heard a loud voice from heaven saying, "Behold, the tabernacle of God is with men, and He will dwell with them, and they shall be His people. God Himself will be with them and be their God. And God will wipe away every tear from their eyes; there shall be no more death, nor sorrow, nor crying. There shall be no more pain, for the former things have passed away." (Revelation 21:3-4)

Prayer

When things go wrong and we cry out to You, help us to become calm and see a way forward.

Prayer for a Sick Infant

David therefore pleaded with God for the child, and David
fasted and went in and lay all night on the ground.
2 Samuel 12:16

As has been stated, David's reign was looked upon as a golden age. Nevertheless David had some serious problems.

As with many great men, David fell into having an affair. He desired Uriah's wife, Bathsheba. Uriah was one of David's leading soldiers. In order to stage a cover-up he manipulated Uriah's death in battle.

The prophet Nathan courageously charged David with this serious sin. David repented, and was forgiven (Psalm 51), but he could not undo what had happened. The king could not escape the serious consequences that were later part of David's subsequent reign.

The adultery led to the birth of a baby boy. Later this little boy became seriously ill. David lay on the ground in anguished prayer, pleading for the infant's life. The answer was, "No." The child died.

Not many have been in David's position. They certainly may not have had a child out of adultery, but they have been faced with the illness of a precious child, knowing that there is a bleak chance of survival. Many have spent long, and terrible nights in prayer but to no avail. God has not restored the child to life and the answer is again, "No."

The shock of loss can be so devastating that it can go on for years. There is not only the loss, but also the seemingly unanswered prayer. There is comfort in the knowledge that each babe who dies is safe with Jesus, but there remains heartache and a gaping void.

We live in a fractured world and none go through life without disappointment, tragedy or bereavement, deserved or undeserved.

Modern medicine, technology and the welfare state have done much to ameliorate the hardship suffered by previous generations, but we cannot totally avoid it. We seem to exchange one measure of problems for another. The words of Jesus are there to comfort the troubled heart.

"Let not your heart be troubled; you believe in God, believe also in Me. In My Father's house are many mansions; if it were not so, I would have told you. I go to prepare a place for you. And if I go and prepare a place for you, I will come again and receive you to Myself; that where I am, there you may be also. And where I go you know, and the way you know."

Thomas said to Him, "Lord, we do not know where You are going, and how can we know the way?"

Jesus said to him, "I am the way, the truth, and the life."
(John 14:1-6)

Prayer

When unexpected disaster strikes the family, may we in our anguish and prayer rest on Your ultimate goodness and mercy.

Prayer for Life

Then he cried out to the Lord and said, "O Lord my God, have
You also brought tragedy on the widow with whom I lodge, by
killing her son?" And he stretched himself out on the child three
times, and cried out to the Lord and said, "O Lord my God, I
pray, let this child's soul come back to him."
1 Kings 17:20-21

During the long centuries of Old Testament history there
are two comparatively short eras when we read of the
miraculous. They were at the time of the Exodus and during
the ministry of Elijah and Elisha. These were periods when
the survival of true religion was in a critical phase.

Elijah was staying in the house of a widow whose whole
means would have depended on her and her son's efforts.
During the prophet's stay the woman's son became gravely
ill and stopped breathing. As with any loss of a child, the
distress would have been intense. Elijah's heart was filled
with a sense of sorrow and urgent enquiry.

Some have believed that Elijah carried out mouth-to-
mouth resuscitation in order to revive the child. (v.21)
Whatever the means, the result was the return of a live boy
to his mother.

The outcome of this incident led to a deepening of the woman's faith. She had seen God at work. As often in Elijah's life it was accompanied with prayer. This time it was urgent and direct.

Prayer for the sick has been a major component of Christian intercession ever since the beginning of the church. It may be the sole act, or it may be associated with medical means as may have been the case here. Medical services have in recent centuries been an important partnership in Christian mission and evangelism in many parts of the world.

On this occasion the widow was blessed with the return of her son. As we have already noted with King David, this was not always the case. We rejoice when healing takes place, but can we still trust Him when it does not? The book of Deuteronomy gives us a helpful insight:

The secret things belong to the Lord our God, but those things which are revealed belong to us and to our children forever, that we may do all the words of this law. (Deuteronomy 29:29)

The Epistle of James gives the church instructions on the matter of healing:

Is anyone among you sick? Let him call for the elders of the church, and let them pray over him, anointing him with oil in the name of the Lord. And the prayer of faith will save the sick, and the Lord will raise him up. (James 5: 14-15)

On reading this passage in James, it says that the Lord will raise him up. The end result may not necessarily be healing of the disease, but certainly that the sick one being prayed for will be saved in eternity. That is something we can hold on to with all our minds and ambition.

Prayer

Lord, we thank You that You care about widows and orphans. Help Your church to be part of that care.

Defeat Turned Round

And he said, "I have been very zealous for the Lord God
of hosts; because the children of Israel have forsaken Your
covenant, torn down Your altars, and killed Your prophets with
the sword. I alone am left; and they seek to take my life."
1 Kings 19:14

Elijah's life and stand for God had been courageous and steadfast. He had obeyed God with unswerving devotion. He had witnessed victory over the pagan prophets at Mount Carmel, but now because of the orders of Queen Jezebel, he was running for his life. He had fallen into depression. He felt that the end of all his labours had resulted in the Israelites' rejection of God's covenant, the destruction of worship centres and the execution of God's prophets. He was the only one left and his cause had failed.

In recent years we have seen the continuing and seemingly inexorable decline of Christianity in Britain and Europe. The march of secularization appears unstoppable. Often we feel that our efforts seem to make little if any difference.

Elijah's feelings can be matched by our own.

God's remedy was to give him some work to do and give Elijah some words of encouragement.

Firstly, Elijah had to leave the place where he was and anoint some future kings. Secondly, God was preparing another, Elisha, to continue the work he had started. Thirdly, God confided that there were still seven thousand in Israel who had not given themselves over to idolatry.

In our own circumstances we have to realize that there are still things to do for God, people to speak to, warn and encourage. We need to remember, as Elijah came to realize, that our God is in control. There are those who have not swallowed the secular creed. There are still God's people, not only in our own country, but millions around the world. His kingdom is advancing in China and other countries of the Far East, Latin America and Africa.

Whatever the future holds for Christian organizations, we know that some will close, some will amalgamate and new ones will rise up. Our job is to see where God is opening doors and go through them.

Elijah got up and carried out his assigned tasks. He did not wallow in his victimhood but recovered from his depression and stayed obedient. It is easy to remain in a state of self-pity, and stay there when an honest prayer and a good treatment programme can be the first move to regaining a sound mind.

For we do not have a High Priest who cannot sympathize with our weaknesses, but was in all points tempted as we are, yet without sin. Let us therefore come boldly to the throne of grace, that we may obtain mercy and find grace to help in time of need. (Hebrews 4:15-16)

Prayer

When we feel discouraged, guide us in the right path never to lose our trust and hope in You.

A Vision of Hope

And when the servant of the man of God arose early and went out, there was an army, surrounding the city with horses and chariots. And his servant said to him, "Alas, my master! What shall we do?"

So he answered, "Do not fear, for those who are with us are more than those who are with them." And Elisha prayed, and said, "Lord, I pray, open his eyes that he may see." Then the Lord opened the eyes of the young man, and he saw. And behold, the mountain was full of horses and chariots of fire all around Elisha.
2 Kings 6:15-17

In this story, the one who prayed was not the desperate one, but the one being prayed for was. The young servant felt that the military situation of the besieged town was hopeless. Elisha wanted him to see the situation as God saw it. When the young man's eyes were opened he saw a massive protective divine army surrounding Elisha.

Many only see the things that are immediately around them; they need spiritual eyes to see the big picture. Many describe their coming to faith as if their eyes suddenly became open. "Though I was blind, now I see." (John 9: 25)

Bertrand Russell, the late famous British philosopher, was asked about his response to God if he found out after death that God really did exist. His reply was, "Sir, there was not enough evidence."

Not only are people spiritually blind, but they refuse to see, even when the evidence is totally sufficient. Paul found similar blindness even in his day.

For since the creation of the world His invisible attributes are clearly seen, being understood by the things that are made, even His eternal power and Godhead, so that they are without excuse, because, although they knew God, they did not glorify Him as God, nor were thankful, but became futile in their thoughts, and their foolish hearts were darkened. Professing to be wise, they became fools. (Romans 1: 20-22)

As well as contending for the faith, we must pray that God will open the blind eyes of both young and old to see the reality of God, and the place and person of Jesus Christ in history and eternity.

Furthermore, those of us who pray need to have our eyes opened to all that God has done and is doing in the world and the life of the church. We need to ask God not what is the most important thing today, but who is the person that God will allow us to meet and is important in His eyes. If we are men and women of prayer, it is funny how God presents us with situations and opportunities to speak about Him. I have often missed opportunities and "messed up", because of spiritual blindness and lack of prayer on my part.

Prayer

Father, help us to see Your work in action. Help us to see even when others cannot.

Prayer for Recovery

In those days Hezekiah was sick and near death. And Isaiah the prophet, the son of Amoz, went to him and said to him, "Thus says the Lord: 'Set your house in order, for you shall die, and not live.'"

Then he turned his face toward the wall, and prayed to the Lord, saying, "Remember now, O Lord, I pray, how I have walked before You in truth and with a loyal heart, and have done what was good in Your sight." And Hezekiah wept bitterly.
2 Kings 20:1-3

Illness can be as painful as it is debilitating. It can be even more harrowing with the knowledge that the disease could be fatal. In his distress, King Hezekiah, prayed and wept. Terminal illness is the great leveller. To those with wealth and power, the best treatment may not be of any use.

Hezekiah was told to, "Set your house in order." Few people are ready for death and few people have all the necessary steps and provisions in place for such a clear eventuality. Many believe that there is nothingness after death, but Christianity teaches that we all have to stand before God.

It seems that Hezekiah suffered a high fever on account of a large abscess. The fig poultice would have been the best treatment of that time. It was probably hot and the sugar solution of the figs would have drawn out and help drain the infection. After that the area would have healed.

Up to that time, Hezekiah, unlike his father Ahaz, had lived a faithful life before God. He lived another fifteen years, but he did not use that time wisely. Foolishly, he showed off the temple treasures to foreign envoys. He also fathered a son, Manasseh, who was evil and perverse. It is suggested that Hezekiah failed to nurture Manasseh in the ways of God.

It is wonderful how God answers Hezekiah's and also our prayers. If for one reason or another, God gives us a longer life than expected, let us use the time well and not fall into arrogance and spiritual decadence. Let us fan the flames of faith and help to advance God's kingdom.

Often, we do not know how or what to pray. The Apostle Paul gives us good advice on this matter:

Likewise the Spirit also helps in our weaknesses. For we do not know what we should pray for as we ought, but the Spirit Himself makes intercession for us with groanings which cannot be uttered. Now He who searches the hearts knows what the mind of the Spirit is, because He makes intercession for the saints according to the will of God. (Romans 8:26-27)

However, God does answer the despairing prayer. Often, during a health crisis God draws close to us and we may be enabled to draw close to Him. Isaiah's command to Hezekiah to set his house in order is not only good advice concerning legal and other matters but a spiritual necessity for us too, in every part of our lives.

Prayer

Dear God, make us aware of Your plans. May we put our future in Your hands and trust in Your abiding love.

When the Odds are Against Us

And Asa cried out to the Lord his God, and said, "Lord, it is nothing for You to help, whether with many or with those who have no power; help us, O Lord our God, for we rest on You, and in Your name we go against this multitude. O Lord, You are our God; do not let man prevail against You!"
2 Chronicles 14:11

Judah was a small and in some ways insignificant nation trapped between competing super-powers to both the North and South. They were under constant threat of invasion and enslavement. Numerically, Judah had little chance of defeating invading armies. The terrain favoured them to some extent but their most significant "weapons" were courage and integrity. That integrity lay in their faith, worship and obedience to the one true God. King Asa, unlike many of his successors, grasped that fact.

When confronted by a massive army from the land south of Egypt, Asa knew that his own military forces were not enough. In this dire situation he prayed to God. A subsequent natural calamity and confusion depleted the invading forces leading to retreat and final defeat. God answered Asa's prayer. Asa uttered this emergency prayer. Although in many ways it was spontaneous, it came out of a trained mind, well versed in the heart and cause of God.

We learn from this that God invites us to pray about national and international political and military situations:

Therefore I exhort first of all that supplications, prayers, intercessions, and giving of thanks be made for all men, for kings and all who are in authority, that we may lead a quiet and peaceable life in all godliness and reverence. For this is good and acceptable in the sight of God our Saviour, who desires all men to be saved and to come to the knowledge of the truth. (1 Timothy 2:1-4)

Asa also realized that as Judah was a nation that worshipped God, the honour of His name was also at stake. The behaviour of Christians and those who purport to be Christians can bring either respect or shame to the church. How often is the name of Christ brought into disrepute by the actions of wayward and lapsed Christians? People will already ridicule us for the sake and offence of the gospel. Let us not add scandal as a reason for persecution.

Do you dishonour God through breaking the law? For "the name of God is blasphemed among the Gentiles because of you, "as it is written. (Romans 2:23-24)

Herbert Lockyer has suggested that how different our civilization would be if we had true Christian nations ruled over by men and women of prayer.

Asa as a king would have had many temptations to backslide. This was something of which the prophet Azariah had to remind even this good king:

"Hear me, Asa, and all Judah and Benjamin. The Lord is with you while you are with Him. If you seek Him, He will be found by you; but if you forsake Him, He will forsake you. For a long time Israel has been without the true God, without a teaching priest, and without law; but when in their trouble they turned to the Lord God of Israel, and sought Him, He was found by them. (2 Chronicles 15:2-4)

We too need reminding of our need to keep spiritually tuned and strong in Christ.

Prayer

Aid us in our trust in You. When obstacles and opposition appear overwhelming, lead us along the right path.

The "Arrow" Prayer

Then the king said to me, "What do you request?"

So I prayed to the God of heaven. And I said to the king, "If it pleases the king, and if your servant has found favour in your sight, I ask that you send me to Judah, to the city of my fathers' tombs, that I may rebuild it."
Nehemiah 2:4-5

Nehemiah was a cupbearer and loyal aide to King Artaxerxes, one of the great pagan kings of Persia. This story highlights the type of relationship that Christians might have with their unbelieving boss. Working for a demanding employer is never easy and this is particularly so when the employer is not a Christian. It is clear that Nehemiah was a man of integrity, trustworthiness, and generally cheerful. He probably did not wear his faith on his sleeve, but there is little doubt that people around him were aware of his religious loyalyies.

Nehemiah was clearly saddened by the news from Jerusalem. The city was still in a state of decay, and repair work was running into many difficulties. Nehemiah believed that he could make a difference.

How would the king respond? Would he be angry?

Would his request make matters worse? We do not know the words Nehemiah used but some things are clear.

Firstly, he knew that God is a God who allows believers to have a personal relationship. Secondly, God accepts and welcomes emergency, and even poorly-worded prayers. Thirdly, God answers prayer.

And so with all that in mind, Nehemiah put his appeal to the king. The king accepted his request, probably because he trusted his servant and knew that in doing so, he would achieve much needed stability in that part of the empire. God's work in the reconstruction of Jerusalem would continue and in response to Nehemiah's prayer, a pagan king became an instrument in the restoration of Israel to a state committed to God. The actions of even unbelieving powerful men and women can enlarge the kingdom of God.

Mao Zedong, the atheist communist dictator, simplified Chinese script and greatly improved literacy in his own country. Little did he realize that in doing so, many more Chinese were able to read the Bible. The growth of Christianity in China has been one of the most significant in the history of the world.

From this brief example, we can be encouraged to pray short arrow prayers in the various situations that we meet every day.

Later, as the task of rebuilding Jerusalem became complete, Nehemiah's cheerfulness and optimism became evident.

"For this day is holy to our Lord. Do not sorrow, for the joy of the Lord is your strength." (Nehemiah 8:10)

God calls us friends. He wants us to pray without ceasing.

No longer do I call you servants, for a servant does not know what his master is doing; but I have called you friends. (John 15:15)

Rejoice always, pray without ceasing, in everything give thanks; for this is the will of God in Christ Jesus for you. (1 Thessalonians 5:16-18)

Do we activate our side of the promise? Do we pray? Do we pray purposefully?

Prayer

Help us to remain close to You so that when facing immediate decisions, we may say and do things which honour You.

We Still Praise God

Then Job arose, tore his robe, and shaved his head; and he fell to
the ground and worshipped. And he said:
"Naked I came from my mother's womb,
And naked shall I return there.
The Lord gave, and the Lord has taken away;
Blessed be the name of the Lord."
Job 1:20-21

The book of Job is of great importance because it deals with questions that have perplexed humankind for centuries. These are the problems of pain, death and seemingly innocent suffering. Job was an upright virtuous man, and yet in the space of a short time he suffered the deaths of loved ones, economic collapse, and his own debilitating illness.

His wife gave the chilling response that Job should curse God and die. (Job 2: 9)

Job, however, did not take the path of the atheist and descend into an accusing abuse. He kept his faith and committed his future to God. He did not react by saying God does not exist, or if He does then He is not all-powerful or He merely does not care. No, in spite of his suffering, He still believed in a creator God, just, loving, all-powerful, and all-knowing. He did not understand the reason and cause of his sad and desperate situation, but this did not alter his fundamental, unshakable belief.

Soon after, some friends came to offer advice, but their advice did not ring true and gave little comfort. If anyone falls into a desperate situation many are quick to blame and state that the sufferer must have done something wrong. Jesus received a similar question:

"Rabbi, who sinned, this man or his parents, that he was born blind?"

Jesus answered, "Neither this man nor his parents sinned, but that the works of God should be revealed in him". (John 9:2-3)

In other words, Jesus said that it is not necessarily right to attribute blame. People may rush to judgment rather than understanding or compassion. We live in a fallen, fractured world. Decay, disease and disaster happen. None are immune.

Job in his perplexed mind kept his belief, and at the end of the book, Job is reminded that God is sovereign, even in calamity.

"Where were you when I laid the foundations of the earth? Tell Me, if you have understanding." (Job 38: 4)

We do not understand all the disasters and misfortunes of the world or individuals. However, God stands by those who trust Him even when everything seems to go wrong. In Job's case he was restored in this life. God may or may not restore us in this life, but He promises us restoration in eternal life.

> *"The Lord gave, and the Lord has taken away;*
> *Blessed be the name of the Lord."*

Prayer

Father, comfort us when we are faced with personal loss so that like Job we may in the end stand secure in the faith of Christ.

The Willing Servant

*In the year that King Uzziah died, I saw the Lord sitting on a
throne, high and lifted up, and the train of His robe filled the
temple. Above it stood seraphim; each one had six wings: with
two he covered his face, with two he covered his feet, and with
two he flew. And one cried to another and said:*

"Holy, holy, holy is the Lord of hosts;

The whole earth is full of His glory!"

*And the posts of the door were shaken by the voice of him who
cried out, and the house was filled with smoke.*

So I said:

"Woe is me, for I am undone!

Because I am a man of unclean lips,

And I dwell in the midst of a people of unclean lips;

For my eyes have seen the King,

The Lord of hosts."…

Also I heard the voice of the Lord, saying:

"Whom shall I send,

And who will go for Us?"

Then I said, "Here am I! Send me."

Isaiah 6:1-8

Isaiah's crisis response was that he was available for

anything that God wanted him to do and be. He had a spectacular dramatic vision of God's power. This was followed by a profound sense of his own unworthiness. Unlike many of God's servants, he said an immediate "Yes" to God's invitation..

As in the case of Moses, it is easy for us to wish that God would send someone else. Alternatively, we might think, "Here am I, send me." The question we need to ask is "Do I want God's best for my life?"

Time after time God's people have descended into negativity. We see the situation around us, and past disappointments and lapsed into a group depression. We can fall into a maintenance survival mode and give little encouragement to those who want to reach out and have new ideas and initiatives. The saying, "Here am I, send me," challenges us to actively serve God. It also demands that we give encouragement and assistance to others who are inspired by God's call.

Isaiah's service and prophecies led many times to a difficult path, but he remained faithful to his calling. His writings are a preview about the coming Jesus Christ, and the substance of the Christian gospel. Isaiah had a profound understanding that Jesus would be a suffering servant and bruised for the sins of the whole world. His prophecies have and still give encouragement to many Christians around the world.

God often gives us work that we never thought we could manage, and abilities we never thought we had. God's people often go through hard times, but with God we have no need to descend into pessimism and cynicism. In the "Acts of the Apostles", Barnabas was a great encourager, are we?

In spite of all his suffering and persecution, Paul put a positive slant on his experience:

"My strength is made perfect in weakness." Therefore most gladly I will rather boast in my infirmities, that the power of Christ may rest upon me. Therefore I take pleasure in infirmities, in reproaches, in needs, in persecutions, in distresses, for Christ's sake. For when I am weak, then I am strong. (2 Corinthians 12:9-10)

Prayer

Father, give us a filling of Your Holy Spirit so that we are able to do whatever You have called us to do.

Too Young?

Then the word of the Lord came to me, saying:
"Before I formed you in the womb I knew you;
Before you were born I sanctified you;
I ordained you a prophet to the nations."
Then said I:
"Ah, Lord God! Behold, I cannot speak, for I am a youth."
Jeremiah 1:4-6

Jeremiah was one of the most significant prophets of the Old Testament. He is known as the weeping prophet. He lived during the time of the collapse of Judah including Jerusalem to the ruthless Babylonians. Although in popular culture he is regarded as a pessimist, he was in fact a realist.

His powerful withering criticism of the idolatry and lack of faithfulness of the southern kingdom and its rulers proved to be true. The consequences of this declension were the fall of Jerusalem, many deaths, the destruction of the temple and thousands taken into exile.

Jeremiah was virtually a lone voice, mocked, abused, imprisoned and persecuted. In spite of all this he remained obstinately faithful. He was despised, but could not be ignored.

At the time of his calling, he was a reluctant appointee. His prayer was instant and easily spat out of his mouth. He made an excuse that he was too young, but God would have none of it. We can only conclude that Jeremiah was forced into service:

> But the Lord said to me:
> "Do not say, 'I am a youth,'
> For you shall go to all to whom I send you,
> And whatever I command you, you shall speak.
> Do not be afraid of their faces,
> For I am with you to deliver you," says the Lord.
> (Jeremiah 1:7-8)

Few of us are called to take the isolated path that Jeremiah walked. Christians normally witness from a base of fellowship with other believers. We work in groups or pairs at the least. We seek affirmation from friends that we are moving in the right direction. We discuss our plans with others. This is right and proper.

However, in rare cases, God calls the one person to speak a hard message for Him. It will be associated with pain and trials, but when God calls, He also equips.

The important foundation is of faith, truth, and the anointing or empowering of the Holy Spirit of God. Although he was reluctant and sometimes seemingly depressed, Jeremiah was grounded in his faith and for the most part, unwavering in his commitment. That can be said of only a few, can it be said of us?

Prayer

Lord, help us to have a right view of our abilities, and never shirk any task that You want us to do.

On Fire for God

Then I said, "I will not make mention of Him,
Nor speak anymore in His name."
But His word was in my heart like a burning fire
Shut up in my bones;
I was weary of holding it back,
And I could not.
Jeremiah 20:9

This verse is part of a larger prayer which summed up Jeremiah's ministry. He was mocked because of his warnings of coming judgment. People awaited his demise. He was almost universally hated. He started by blaming God for his difficulties, and yet, in spite of all this trauma and hardship, he could not restrain his message. God's prophecies were inside him like a fire! Even if he tried, Jeremiah could not hold back. That was the desperate nature of his prayer. I do not think that Jeremiah had a natural fiery impulsive personality. His fire came from a deep inner conviction given by God.

Later in his prayer, Jeremiah turned from blame to praise.

In every day and age, God needs people who are on

fire for Him. I remember taking a Polish priest to a church in Sheffield. On hearing the sermon, he said, "Fire, fire, I want fire!"

His English was limited, and he probably understood little, but he could detect fire, the fire of the Spirit, and that is what he wanted in his own ministry.

Jeremiah's ministry resulted in possibly one conversion. The prophecy written in the Old Testament has inspired many successful evangelistic sermons.

Jeremiah remained faithful to the end, but his persecution did not cease.

According to tradition, he was taken to Egypt by escapees from the fall of Jerusalem. He was a prisoner and subsequently murdered.

His was not a life of comfort but one of faithfulness and suffering. No doubt he was one of the faithful referred to by the author of the Epistle to the Hebrews.

Still others had trial of mockings and scourgings, yes, and of chains and imprisonment. They were stoned, they were sawn in two, were tempted, were slain with the sword. They wandered about in sheepskins and goatskins, being destitute, afflicted, tormented - of whom the world was not worthy. They wandered in deserts and mountains, in dens and caves of the earth. (Hebrews 11:36-38)

We all come to Christ in different ways. We have the great privilege of having a glimpse of the Lord's joy. We may experience suffering, but Jesus still advises us to be cheerful because He has overcome the world. (John 16: 33)

Prayer

May the knowledge of Your presence set our hearts on fire to love and serve You always.

Do Not Be Afraid!

Now when He got into a boat, His disciples followed Him. And suddenly a great tempest arose on the sea, so that the boat was covered with the waves. But He was asleep. Then His disciples came to Him and awoke Him, saying, "Lord, save us! We are perishing!"

And Peter answered Him and said, "Lord, if it is You, command me to come to You on the water."

So He said, "Come." And when Peter had come down out of the boat, he walked on the water to go to Jesus. But when he saw that the wind was boisterous, he was afraid; and beginning to sink he cried out, saying, "Lord, save me!"
Matthew 8:23-27, and Matthew 14:28-30

These two passages concern danger at sea. The first one is associated with possible drowning as a result of a storm, and the second is possible drowning after Peter tried to walk on the water. They both contain the despairing words, "Lord, save us", or "Lord, save me".

Even a person who has barely ever given God a thought up to that point of grave danger will often utter the words, " God save me!" In the first case the storm was abated, and in the second, Jesus pulled Peter out of the sea.

The name Jesus means "Saviour", and in these cases Jesus saved His people from drowning. On other occasions, the disciples saw people saved from diseases, their demon possession, their greed and multiple problems. Many look on religion as a means to sort out their life's difficulties. That often happens, and many Christians can testify how God has intervened wonderfully in many of life's seemingly hopeless situations. These include areas of health, work, relationships and family tensions.

Nevertheless, Christianity is not a mere code of ethics or a sophisticated lucky charm. The disciples eventually came to understand the truth of this. As Jesus' ministry unfolded, culminating in the cross, resurrection and post-resurrection teaching, the disciples came to a complete understanding of the terms, "being saved", and "salvation'.

On the first day of Pentecost, Peter in his sermon used the term 'save', and 'saved':

> *And it shall come to pass*
> *That whoever calls on the name of the Lord*
> *Shall be saved.* (Acts 2:21)

The meaning of saved involves repentance, faith, and extends from now to eternity. This is being saved from sin, death and hell. What a wonderful promise and outcome!

The words, 'salvation' and 'saved' are important and numerous in the New Testament. They are so important that we are implored not to ignore them.

The price of disregard is devastating and the writer to the Hebrews urged this on his readers:

Therefore we must give the more earnest heed to the things we have heard, lest we drift away. For if the word spoken through angels proved steadfast, and every transgression and disobedience received a just reward, how shall we escape if we neglect so great a salvation, which at the first began to be spoken by the Lord, and was confirmed to us by those who heard Him... (Hebrews 2:1-3)

Prayer

Lord, we thank You that You desire that none should perish but that all should come to a knowledge of the Truth. Make us embrace Your Truth for Jesus' sake, who is the Truth.

Help Me To Believe

*Immediately the father of the child cried out and said with tears,
"Lord, I believe; help my unbelief!"*
Mark 9:24

This cry from a man in distress about his son's apparent demon possession and epilepsy has been repeated in every generation. It is a massive trial to cope with family illness or disability, especially that of a child. In this case, the demon was exorcized and the boy was healed.

For us, the problems sometimes go away or recede, but often they persist, day after day, year after year. Sometimes we manage to come to terms with the situation and sometimes we do not.

We live in a broken, fallen world. Even with modern medicine and technology, numerous clinical challenges and tragedies remain. Many feel that their faith is stretched to the limit and that they are just holding on by their fingernails.

In these circumstances, in spite of all our difficulties and lack of faith, we become aware that God is still carrying us on. We become survivors and others find encouragement on seeing how God's faithful people manage in the most desperate situations.

There are no easy answers, but even with a mere strand of faith, God comes into our lives.

In spite of all our trials, disappointments and partial belief, we can be encouraged in God.

God does not promise immunity from the problems humankind has to face and suffer, but He does promise a coping mechanism, He does promise not to test us more than we can cope with.

Jesus answered them, "Do you now believe? Indeed the hour is coming, yes, has now come, that you will be scattered, each to his own, and will leave Me alone. And yet I am not alone, because the Father is with Me. These things I have spoken to you, that in Me you may have peace. In the world you will have tribulation; but be of good cheer, I have overcome the world." (John 16:31-33)

Whatever faith we have, let us use it in the service of God. We must not delay until our faith is more perfect or more like that of another believer. We can still glorify God; we can still be part of His plan.

As far as our unbelief is concerned, we can say the words of this distressed man, "Help my unbelief." To ask for help, even in unbelief, is a cry of faith. Let us resist unbelief, pray against it, and not let it keep us from seeking Christ with our whole heart.

Prayer
Forgive our lack of faith, and guide us to trust in You fully.

If Only You Had Been Here

Now Martha said to Jesus, "Lord, if You had been here, my brother would not have died."
John 11:21

A death in the family is devastating to the relatives, particularly to those who are close. An untimely death seems even the more shocking. Those who are affected can go through periods of anger, denial, blame, bargaining, depression and many other emotions.

Martha, Mary, and Lazarus lived at a home in Bethany, not far from Jerusalem. They were a reasonably well-to-do family and they were delighted to use their home and means to extend hospitality to Jesus and His disciples. It was an open house. They, unlike others, were not selfish in the use of their possessions. Jesus often loved to stay there. It could be described as a believing, loyal household.

Martha was, in a sense, blaming Jesus for her brother's death.

We often hear complaints against God for the loss of loved ones. "If God really cared then I would not have lost my daughter!" – or any other close friend or relative. This can sometimes be associated with loss of any belief in

God, "He did not care about me, so I am not going to have anything to do with your God!"

In Martha's case, she, in her grief and puzzlement, still hung on to her faith in Jesus. In doing so, she was told of a wonderful and profound truth about the resurrection. "Your brother will rise again." (John 11: 23)

The death of a close one can drive people away from God or draw us closer to Him.

Jesus then uttered profound words that have brought comfort to millions:

Jesus said to her, "I am the resurrection and the life. He who believes in Me, though he may die, he shall live. And whoever lives and believes in Me shall never die. Do you believe this?"

She said to Him, "Yes, Lord, I believe that You are the Christ, the Son of God, who is to come into the world."

Jesus honoured and proved these words in the raising of Lazarus and His own subsequent resurrection. They were not empty words but were accompanied with life and power.

We often go through many emotions in coping with the deaths of our nearest and dearest. Furthermore, we have to face the prospect of our own death and the possible surrounding circumstances.

We can rest assured that the Resurrection of Jesus and His all-encompassing and enveloping love will give us all the comfort and reassurance in times of extreme need. Even with modern medicine, the human resources and technology available to us, we will all have to face bereavement and our own mortality.

Prayer

Lord Jesus, we thank You that through the resurrection You conquered death and opened the gate of Heaven.

Prayer in a Garden

He went a little farther and fell on His face, and prayed,
saying, "O My Father, if it is possible, let this cup pass from
Me; nevertheless, not as I will, but as You will."
Matthew 26:39

The prayers of Jesus were not desperate in the sense that we might regard as desperate. It is impossible for us to understand the deep relationship within the Trinity, but we know that there is a sublime communion. In this instance, Luke's Gospel tells us that Jesus at this moment of anguish sweated drops of blood. Although it was not a desperate prayer, it was a prayer uttered in a crisis.

Even at this moment the disciples were unable to sit with Jesus and even fell asleep.

Jesus knew He was about to suffer a criminal's death on a cross. He was aware of the pain and anguish of this barbaric method of execution. Could another way be found which did not involve this utterly hideous and disgusting method of torture. Then, He committed Himself to His Father's will.

Jesus knew that His death would be the means of forgiveness for millions and that He would be the one to pay the price of sin. He would take the penalty off us and receive it to Himself. In doing so, for the first time in His life, He would experience separation from His Father. He who knew no sin was to be made sin for us. It is generally agreed that it was the prospect of separation from His Father, whilst on the cross, that grieved Him the most.

Some have felt that that God could have forgiven sins without the cross, and have even called the cross, cosmic child abuse. It is impossible to give a full treatment of this issue in these short comments, but such a view tends to neglect the utter holiness of God and also the terrible nature of human sin. Love is at the heart of the triune Godhead, Father, Son, and Holy Spirit. At the cross God's wrath was turned from us onto His beloved Son.

And as Moses lifted up the serpent in the wilderness, even so must the Son of Man be lifted up, that whoever believes in Him should not perish but have eternal life. For God so loved the world that He gave His only begotten Son, that whoever believes in Him should not perish but have everlasting life. For God did not send His Son into the world to condemn the world, but that the world through Him might be saved. (John 3:14-17)

After the prayer of anguish Jesus got up, gently admonished His disciples, and then with great courage and commitment faced His betrayer.

We will never understand the full nature of Jesus' anguish, but when we pray in a crisis situation, we can get up and with God's help face the imminent trial and pain.

Prayer

Forgive our proud hearts and turn our wills to be conformed to Your gracious and loving will.

A Dying Thief

But the other, answering, rebuked him, saying, "Do
you not even fear God, seeing you are under the same
condemnation? And we indeed justly, for we receive the
due reward of our deeds; but this Man has done nothing
wrong." Then he said to Jesus, "Lord, remember me when You
come into Your kingdom." And Jesus said to him, "Assuredly, I
say to you, today you will be with Me in Paradise."
Luke 23:40-43

The cross of Jesus is a subject of profound significance.
During this time of dreadful execution, our Lord, as ever
during His ministry, concerned Himself with the needs
of others. The two thieves either side of Jesus joined the
crowds and the leading authorities in their taunts and
mockery.

Then one of the thieves, in desperation, had a change of
heart.

He realized that he was guilty and that Jesus was
innocent. Not only was Jesus innocent, He was also their
King. We do not know how clear the thief's understanding
was about our Lord's status and person, but it was clear
enough for him to speak the words, "Lord, remember

me." Jesus responded to this cry of faith by promising the undeserving thief life with Him in Paradise.

It is one of the wonders and paradoxes of Christianity that the most dreadful of humanity can be saved. Conversely, the most upright and apparently moral but rejecters of Christ are in danger of eternal Hell.

A previous jibe against Jesus was:

And the Pharisees and the scribes complained, saying, "This Man receives sinners and eats with them." (Luke 15:2)

There are countless testimonies of people who have come to Christ from the most appalling backgrounds and circumstances. God seems to choose and accept the most unlikely people. Criminals who have committed the most extreme crimes have become Christians whilst in prison. Some of these conversions have been false, but many have been transforming and genuine.

The most sobering fact is that all who come to Christ must come to Him in the same way as this shameful, crucified thief. We all have to accept our responsibility of guilt. We all have to ask to be remembered by our King, the Son of God.

For He made Him who knew no sin to be sin for us, that we might become the righteousness of God in Him. (2 Corinthians 5:21)

Prayer

Thank You, Father, that You give eternal life to all who turn to You whatever the circumstance whatever the guilt.

The Saviour of the World

And about the ninth hour Jesus cried out with a loud voice,
saying, "Eli, Eli, lama sabachthani?" that is, "My God, My
God, why have You forsaken Me?"
Matthew 27:46

First of all, although this short prayer appears to be desperate, it is not so when looked at in the whole context of Jesus' prayer in the garden of Gethsemane and subsequent trial and events leading to the cross. Jesus still trusted His Father.

Just as David uttered this cry of anguish, (Psalm 22: 1) so does David's Greater Son.

In the case of Jesus, His desolation is linked to that time on the cross when He was cut off from His Father. Sin separates, and in carrying the world's penalty, including our penalty for sin on that cross, Jesus was forsaken.

It is interesting that both Matthew and Luke follow the death of Jesus with the record of the temple curtain being torn in two from the top to the bottom. This signified that the barrier of sin that was between humankind and God had been broken.

Christians have often faced the most extreme conditions both in forms of persecution and otherwise. Accounts of martyrdom have often described the wonder and glorious sense of God's presence and tangible support to God's people during the most violent instances. An example of that is found in the case of Stephen. (Acts 7: 54-60) We wonder how we would react in similar circumstances.

Other Christians have known severe clinical depression and even committed suicide under feelings of forsakenness. Even the most even temperaments suffer the anguish of bereavement, the grievous disappointment in unfulfilled expectation, and the seemingly unanswered prayer. Many have prayed for certain good things for their family members and the opposite has happened.

Our reaction is often that of disappointment, anger and a feeling that God does not care. Many have lost the faith that they thought they once had, whilst others have been driven closer to God.

We need to ask ourselves the question, "Have I become a believer in order to have an easier life and be protected from the misfortunes of this world?" Or, "Am I a Christian because I have been forgiven and am now safe for eternity and that He will be for us for whatever our needs?" If we are a believer for the first reason, then we will certainly be disillusioned. If for the second reason, then we can rest on the promises of God.

Jesus disappointed His critics for numerous reasons. John tells us that after His discourse on the bread of life, many followers left Jesus and went their own way. They were clearly shocked at the symbol of eating Christ's flesh and drinking His blood. They could not understand that we receive Christ by faith. The first century Israelites wanted a Messiah who would bring in a new political golden age of prosperity, and all the teaching about bread and eating Jesus' flesh baffled and disillusioned them.

As they walked away and a few were left standing:

And He said, "Therefore I have said to you that no one can come to Me unless it has been granted to him by My Father."

From that time many of His disciples went back and walked with Him no more. Then Jesus said to the twelve, "Do you also want to go away?"

But Simon Peter answered Him, "Lord, to whom shall we go? You have the words of eternal life. Also we have come to believe and know that You are the Christ, the Son of the living God." (John 6:65-69)

Well said, Peter! We all have spiritual highs and lows. When we are at our lowest and feeling the most forsaken it is then we still say, "My God….." He is still our God who clings on to us as we cling on to Him.

Prayer

We thank You, Father, that when Jesus was forsaken, He bore the penalty for all our sins on that dreadful cross. Help us to know the victory over sin that You secured.

Christic is Risen!

"Sir, if You have carried Him away, tell me where You have laid Him, and I will take Him away."
John 20:15

Mary Magdalene was in a state of huge shock and bereavement following Jesus' death on the cross. Jesus had sorted out her life and cleared her of her demons.

She with other women and the disciples had enormous expectations about the future. All these had been cruelly dashed. All she could hope for was a life of memories and the remains of Jesus which might be a focus of pilgrimage.

She then came face to face with the risen Christ. She was a witness of that momentous event. The resurrection of Jesus confirmed that everything Jesus said and did was true. Death was and is defeated and each Christian has an everlasting hope. Mary was the first to see it and it needs remembering that God gave this privilege to a woman.

Great men and women have their tombs which are visited by thousands and millions. Karl Marx has his grave in Highgate cemetery and both Lenin and Mao Zedong have their mausoleums. The tombs of these secular materialists are occupied by bones, but Jesus' tomb remains empty.

Since then the message and good news of hope has gone around the world.

"Christ is risen!"

Today, some come tentatively to Christ. They may utter a prayer very similar in tone to that of Mary Magdalene. "God, if You really are there, I don't know what to believe about Jesus. I don't know if He is alive, but if He is, show me!"

Many who have begun with this faltering prayer have been rewarded by a growing conviction about the truth of Christ. C. S. Lewis the Christian author and teacher had a similar journey and finally on his conversion described himself as the world's most reluctant convert.

Mary's meeting with Jesus was followed by that of the Disciples.

Then the disciples were glad when they saw the Lord. (John 20:20)

The word, "Glad," was an understatement. They were overjoyed!

May we all have John 20:20 vision and have our faith in the risen Lord.

Prayer

Lord Jesus, we thank You that You defied death in rising on that wonderful first day of the week, early while it was still dark. May we rejoice in Your victory every day.

A Momentous Question

And he said, "Who are You, Lord?"
Acts 9:5

Saul of Tarsus was one of the most brilliant intellects of his generation. He was dynamic, imaginative and energetic. He was also very arrogant about his education and his status as a Pharisee. He was consumed by hatred towards Christians. He had a warped willingness to see them persecuted and murdered. He was proud that he was the ringleader in this vicious enterprise. He went from house to house dragging Messianic believers off to prison.

He travelled with a group to Damascus in order to arrest believers and bring them back for trial and sentence in Jerusalem.

Then he had a vision near Damascus when he saw a great blinding light. He heard a voice, "Saul, Saul, why are you persecuting Me?"

In desperation he blurted out, "Who are you, Lord?" It was his first real effective prayer and the answer shattered Him. "I am Jesus, whom you are persecuting."

The one whom he did not know, the one whom he

thought was an imposter, the one whom he had hated was the person of his vision.

From then on Saul's life changed. He remained the brilliant dynamo, but he was turned from a man of hate to a man of love, from a man of pride to a man of humility.

Rejoice in Christ Jesus, and have no confidence in the flesh, though I also might have confidence in the flesh. If anyone else thinks he may have confidence in the flesh, I more so: circumcised the eighth day, of the stock of Israel, of the tribe of Benjamin, a Hebrew of the Hebrews; concerning the law, a Pharisee; concerning zeal, persecuting the church; concerning the righteousness which is in the law, blameless.

But what things were gain to me, these I have counted loss for Christ. Yet indeed I also count all things loss for the excellence of the knowledge of Christ Jesus my Lord, for whom I have suffered the loss of all things, and count them as rubbish, that I may gain Christ. (Philippians 3:3-8)

Our experience will very rarely be as dramatic as that of Saul, but as we are challenged by the gospel we have to come to the moment when we pray those simple words, "Who are You, Lord?" The word, "Lord," takes us to the point of saying, "Yes!", to the reply that it is Jesus. We all have to come to a moment of declaring to ourselves and to others what we think of Jesus. Are you going to say that I do not want Him in my life, I want to go my own way, I know better? Conversely, do you want to say, "Yes!", to all He is and all He wants for you? Our response to this question is the most important we will ever make.

Prayer

Lord, we thank You that You reveal Yourself to the most unlikely people. We pray that even the most stubborn and resistant are able to come into Your kingdom.

A Thorn in the Flesh

And lest I should be exalted above measure by the abundance of the revelations, a thorn in the flesh was given to me, a messenger of Satan to buffet me, lest I be exalted above measure. Concerning this thing I pleaded with the Lord three times that it might depart from me.
2 Corinthians 12:7-8

We do not know what Paul's "thorn in the flesh" was. Some have said it was a relapsing fever. Others have suggested epilepsy or even persecution from his fellow countrymen. The most likely cause was an eye complaint. He referred to this in his Epistle to the Galatians. (Galatians 4:15)

Three times he prayed desperately for it to go away but it never did. Paul, who had been an agent in signs and wonders, and such blessing to others had to continue to suffer.

Many of us have chronic and often painful conditions which go on and on. We can have bad days and better days but it never seems to go away. We pray about it, we consult doctors, we take medication, but nothing seems to work completely.

We have to face the fact that normally a patient or loved one with advanced cancer or dementia will not get better. Our prayers need to be towards God's sufficient grace to manage the last years, months and days with joy and even a sense of victory. It is a tough but necessary truth.

We are in the same position as Paul.

He was told that God's grace was sufficient for him. He then came to a startling conclusion:

Therefore most gladly I will rather boast in my infirmities, that the power of Christ may rest upon me. Therefore I take pleasure in infirmities, in reproaches, in needs, in persecutions, in distresses, for Christ's sake. For when I am weak, then I am strong. (2 Corinthians 12:9-10)

It seems that in this case, Paul's condition with God's sufficient grace made him even more powerful in God's cause of the gospel.

Paul saw God's grace on many levels. It concerned his call to be a Christian and Apostle. It was there for day-to-day guidance. It was principally present for his and the church's ultimate destiny.

For he who sows to his flesh will of the flesh reap corruption, but he who sows to the Spirit will of the Spirit reap everlasting life. And let us not grow weary while doing good, for in due season we shall reap if we do not lose heart. Therefore, as we have opportunity, let us do good to all, especially to those who are of the household of faith. (Galatians 6:8-10)

There are many who care for both young and older relatives. We spend vast amounts of physical and emotional energy. In the challenge and sometimes heartache, let us be faithful in both our caring and calling.

Prayer

We thank You that we will not be tested more than we can bear. Help us to rejoice in all Your grace and blessing.

Christ Will Come Again

He who testifies to these things says, "Surely I am coming quickly."

Amen. Even so, come, Lord Jesus!
Revelation 22:20

When John wrote the final book of the Bible, the world was in turmoil. All the other apostles had died and as far as we know they all died violently at the hands of their persecutors. Christians had been martyred in their thousands. They were put to death for the entertainment of the emperor and the masses.

The mighty Roman army had reduced Jerusalem to rubble and the temple had been destroyed so that not one stone stood on another. (Matthew 24:2)

This turmoil was reflected in the vivid disturbing imagery of John's powerful writing.

Such was the overwhelming persecution that many thought that the second coming of Jesus was imminent.

There was a sense of hope as well as despair. And so the final prayer of the Bible is short with a longing, loving expectation of the coming of Jesus. Every wrong will be put right. All God's people will be with Him. All the old things with their hurts and sorrows will be gone. There will be no more crying, no more separation from God.

Contemporary cities were exciting places with commerce and community, but they were all tainted with cruelty and corruption. There will be a new Heaven and a new Earth. The heavenly city will be beautiful and a joy to inhabit. No wonder those first century Christians longed for Christ's return.

There were some including scoffers who wondered and were deeply concerned about the apparent delay. "Where is the promise of His coming?" (2 Peter 3:4)

Peter answered this criticism and concern with very wise words:

But, beloved, do not forget this one thing, that with the Lord one day is as a thousand years, and a thousand years as one day. The Lord is not slack concerning His promise, as some count slackness, but is longsuffering toward us, not willing that any should perish but that all should come to repentance. (2 Peter 3:8-9)

Peter points out that we need to wait until all God's people have been called and come to trust in Him. I am glad that He has waited long enough for peoples from every nation including ourselves to be brought into His Kingdom. In a way the coming of Jesus is immanent. In another way we wait till everyone of His people is finally secure.

Amen, even so, come, Lord Jesus!

Prayer

As we live each day in Your service, may we be expectant of Your coming in glory.

Desperate Prayer